Chimidyue

A Folktale of the Amazon Rainforest

Retold by Leslie Falconer
Pictures by Chris Lensch

To Kristen, it's a jungle
out there. Thanks for helping
me find my way. – C.L.

To Eliana Elias and Minga Peru, who
taught me about the mysteries of the
Amazon Rainforest. – L.F.

First published by Experience Early Learning Company
7243 Scotchwood Lane, Grawn, Michigan 49637 USA

Text Copyright © 2014 by Experience Early Learning Co.
Manufactured in No.8, Yin Li Street, Tian He District, Guangzhou,
Guangdong, China by Sun Fly Printing Limited
4th Printing 01/2023

ISBN: 978-1-937954-17-8
Visit us at www.ExperienceEarlyLearning.com

Chimidyue lived with her family in a big house called a maloca. Every day the boys would run off with the men to fish and hunt. Chimidyue watched them disappear into the thick rainforest. She stayed home and made baskets. She did not dare enter the rainforest. It was filled with fierce animals and scary sounds.

One day while Chimidyue wove a basket, she saw a big, beautiful morpho butterfly dancing before her. The sunlight sparkled on its blue wings. "You are the most magical creature in the world," Chimidyue said dreamingly. "I wish I could be like you."

The butterfly fluttered near Chimidyue's eyes and then flew to the edge of the forest. Chimidyue set down her basket and followed the butterfly. They danced and twirled and leaped deeper and deeper into the forest. She played for a long time with the butterfly. Then, the butterfly flew between two vines and disappeared.

Chimidyue stopped.
She was lost.
She had gone too far
into the rainforest.

What was she going to do?

Chimidyue heard a noise that made a quick tap, tap, tap. It sounded like someone working in the forest. But when she walked around a large tree, she found a woodpecker.
"Please show me the way out of the forest," Chimidyue pleaded.

Tap
Tap
Tap
Tap

"No!" the woodpecker said with anger. "Why should I make time for you? Your people cut down the trees and stole my home. I'm much too busy building a new place to live."

Tears fell from Chimidyue's eyes. Through her blurry tears, she looked ahead and saw a woman sitting on a tree stump. "Oh, Grandmother," Chimidyue said, "I have lost my way. I'm so scared. Which way should I go?"

"Don't say 'grandmother' to me!" shouted the woman. But when Chimidyue neared the tree stump, she realized it was just a tinamou bird. The tinamou squawked, "How many of my kind have your people hunted and chased through the forest?" With that the tinamou ran off on her short, strong legs and left Chimidyue standing alone.

Then, something dropped on Chimidyue's head. She looked up and saw a group of spider monkeys eating genipa. They waved at Chimidyue and started swinging from vine to vine. Chimidyue ran after them. *What silly animals, she thought.*

"Come to our festival! We will dance all night!" they exclaimed.

As Chimidyue followed them, she heard the sounds of beating drums and rattling sticks growing stronger and stronger. Chimidyue watched it all in wonder and smiled as she danced with her monkey friends. It was just like the festivals of her people. Then, she noticed the eyes of a big monkey watching her in the shadows. She shivered.

These eyes were not friendly. She stepped closer to the shadows and saw it was not a monkey at all. It was a beast with black spots and a fierce body.

"Jaguar!" Chimidyue gasped.

She ran away from the monkey festival
and quietly slipped amongst the roots of
a kapok tree to hide.

"I do not understand anything in the forest," she sobbed. "Nothing is as it appears."

Suddenly, she heard the whisper of butterfly wings. The blue morpho had returned!

"Dear Chimidyue," said the morpho gently, "in your village, life is simple. But surrounding you is a place much bigger and filled with many mysteries. This is the way of the forest."

"How will I ever find my way home?" asked Chimidyue.

"Follow me," said the butterfly.

Chimidyue danced and twirled and leaped with the butterfly once again until she arrived just outside of the rainforest. She stood on the banks of the Amazon. Chimidyue could see her village was on the other side. "I crossed the river without knowing it? How will I ever get back?"

"Close your eyes and dream that you are a butterfly," whispered the blue morpho. Chimidyue closed her eyes.

She dreamed that she was the most beautiful butterfly in the rainforest!

When Chimidyue opened her eyes, she was on the other side of the river. "I want to be a butterfly like you forever!" she exclaimed.

"That would not be right," said the butterfly, "as you belong with your people. They love you and care for you. Do not worry. Now that you have been with us, you will always have a piece of the forest within you."

Chimidyue waved good-bye and skipped home with a heart that had the wings of a butterfly.

The End

About the story

Chimidyue (chim-ID-yoo-a)

Chimidyue's story is from the Takuna tribe of South America. The Takuna live in the upper Amazon River area. They have a rich tradition of storytelling. The tale of Chimidyue is unique because it features a female as the main character.

Key vocabulary

Grandmother, Grandfather: a term of respect for elders.

Genipa (JEN-ip-a): a green fruit with a colorless juice that turns black when it dries. Some people use the juice as a skin dye.

Kapok (KAY-pock): a tree with large root systems. Some Amazonians believe that this large rainforest tree has a soul.

Maloca (mul-O-ka): a large house where all of the relatives live. A maloca may be up to 50 ft wide and 100 ft long. A long time ago, malocas were oval-shaped with walls to keep away the insects. Now, they may not have walls and instead use mosquito nets to keep out the insects.

Morpho (MOR-fo): a large tropical butterfly with blue wings

experience
EARLY LEARNING

Experience Early Learning specializes in the development and publishing of research-based curriculum, books, music and authentic assessment tools for early childhood teachers and parents around the world. Our mission is to inspire children to experience learning through creative expression, play and open-ended discovery. We believe educational materials that invite children to participate with their whole self (mind, body and spirit) support on-going development and encourage children to become the authors of their own unique learning stories.

www.ExperienceEarlyLearning.com